PRAYERS & PROMISES
for

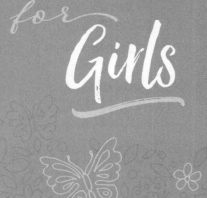
Girls

BroadStreet
KIDS

CONTENTS

Introduction

It is a wonderful blessing to be a daughter of God! You can take great joy in knowing that he made you special and he wants a relationship with you. Reading even just a little bit of his Word each day will make you smile and fill you with hope.

Prayers & Promises for Girls is a topically organized collection of God's promises that guide you through lessons of beauty, confidence, love, joy, wisdom, and more. Heartfelt prayers and prompting questions give you an opportunity to think more deeply about the promises found in God's Word.

Be encouraged as you sit with God and learn more about the love he has for you!

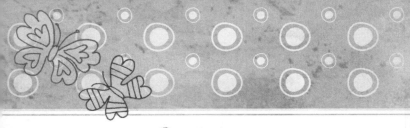

Confidence

I can do everything through Christ,
who gives me strength.

PHILIPPIANS 4:13 NLT

Be my rock of refuge,
to which I can always go;
give the command to save me,
for you are my rock and my fortress....
For you have been my hope, Sovereign LORD,
my confidence since my youth.

PSALM 71:3, 5 NIV

The LORD will be at your side.
He will keep your feet from being caught in a trap.

PROVERBS 3:26 NIRV

Dear God, I don't always feel confident in myself. Comparing myself to others hurts sometimes. Help me not to think this way because with you, I don't need to be anyone else. Please give me the confidence I need to stand up tall every day.

How does Jesus make you feel confident?

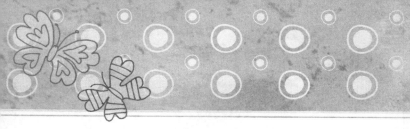

Blessings

Surely, Lord, you bless those who do what is right.
Like a shield, your loving care keeps them safe.

PSALM 5:12 NIRV

Surely you have granted him unending blessings
and made him glad with the joy of your presence.

PSALM 21:6 NIV

"Even more blessed are all who hear the word of God and
put it into practice."

LUKE 11:28 NLT

Give praise to the God and Father of our Lord Jesus
Christ. He has blessed us with every spiritual blessing.
Those blessings come from the heavenly world. They
belong to us because we belong to Christ. God chose us to
belong to Christ before the world was created. He chose
us to be holy and without blame in his eyes. He loved us.

EPHESIANS 1:3-4 NIRV

Dear God, thank you for everything you have given me.
I have a happy heart because of the friends you have put in
my life and the fun times you let me have. I pray I will use the
blessings in my life to honor you.

What gifts has God blessed you with lately?

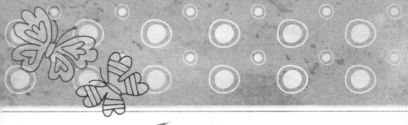

Forgiveness

"If you forgive other people when they sin against you,
your heavenly Father will also forgive you."

MATTHEW 6:14 NIV

Put up with each other. Forgive one another if you are
holding something against someone. Forgive, just as the
Lord forgave you.

COLOSSIANS 3:13 NIRV

God is faithful and fair. If we confess our sins, he will
forgive our sins. He will forgive every wrong thing we
have done. He will make us pure.

1 JOHN 1:9 NIRV

He is so rich in kindness and grace that he purchased our
freedom with the blood of his Son and forgave our sins.

EPHESIANS 1:7 NLT

Dear God, it's not always easy to forgive others. Sometimes my friends are mean to me, and I don't feel like making peace. Please help me to forgive others just as you forgave me.

Who do you need to forgive today?

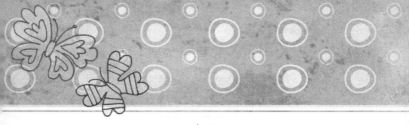

Hope

The Lord is good to those whose hope is in him,
to the one who seeks him.

LAMENTATIONS 3:25 NIV

Hope will never bring us shame. That's because God's
love has poured into our hearts. This happened through
the Holy Spirit, who has been given to us.

ROMANS 5:5 NIRV

The Lord's delight is in those who fear him,
those who put their hope in his unfailing love.

PSALM 147:11 NLT

Dear God, thank you for giving me hope that is alive. Jesus died for me and gave me the gift of the Holy Spirit. Guide me to seek you in everything I do because I know that you will never let me down.

Knowing that God is always there for you, what can you be hopeful for?

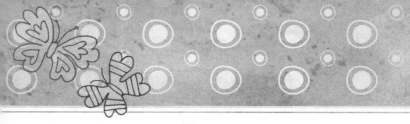

Peace

"I have told you these things, so that you can have peace
because of me. In this world you will have trouble. But be
encouraged! I have won the battle over the world."

JOHN 16:33 NIRV

The LORD gives his people strength.
The LORD blesses them with peace.

PSALM 29:11 NLT

May the Lord of peace himself give you peace at all times
and in every way. The Lord be with all of you.

2 THESSALONIANS 3:16 NIV

"I am leaving you with a gift—peace of mind and heart.
And the peace I give is a gift the world cannot give.
So don't be troubled or afraid."

JOHN 14:27 NLT

Dear God, thank you for the gift of peace. I have peace in my mind and my heart. I know this is of you and not the world. In times of trouble, help me to remember that you have already won the battle.

What does peace look like for you?

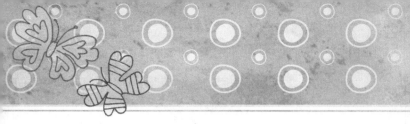

Salvation

"This is how God loved the world: He gave his one and only Son, so that everyone who believes in him will not perish but have eternal life."

JOHN 3:16 NLT

For the wages of sin is death, but the gift of God is eternal life in Christ Jesus our Lord.

ROMANS 6:23 NIV

God's grace has saved you because of your faith in Christ. Your salvation doesn't come from anything you do. It is God's gift.

EPHESIANS 2:8 NIRV

If you openly declare that Jesus is Lord and believe in your heart that God raised him from the dead, you will be saved.

ROMANS 10:9 NLT

Dear Jesus, thank you for dying on the cross for me. I know that I am a sinner, and you are the only way to eternal life in heaven. I want to give you my whole heart so that I can be with you always.

Do you know what it means to be saved?

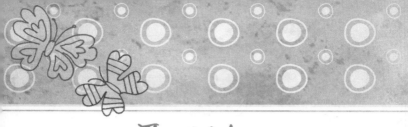

Thankfulness

I have not stopped giving thanks for you,
remembering you in my prayers.

EPHESIANS 1:16 NIV

Giving thanks is a sacrifice that truly honors me.
If you keep to my path,
I will reveal to you the salvation of God.

PSALM 50:23 NLT

Rejoice always, pray continually,
give thanks in all circumstances;
for this is God's will for you in Christ Jesus.

1 THESSALONIANS 5:16–18 NIV

Give thanks as you enter the gates of his temple.
Give praise as you enter its courtyards.
Give thanks to him and praise his name.

PSALM 100:4 NIRV

Dear God, you are so good! Thank you for this day. Thank you for my friends and family. Help me to give you thanks in all I do and say. You are the reason for all the blessings in my life.

What can you thank God for right now?

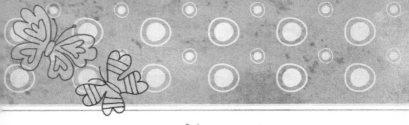

Worry

Turn your worries over to the LORD.
He will keep you going.
He will never let godly people be shaken.

PSALM 55:22 NIRV

"Who of you by worrying
can add a single hour to your life?"

LUKE 12:25 NIV

Worry weighs a person down;
an encouraging word cheers a person up.

PROVERBS 12:25 NLT

Do not worry about anything, but pray and ask God for
everything you need, always giving thanks. And God's
peace, which is so great we cannot understand it, will
keep your hearts and minds in Christ Jesus.

PHILIPPIANS 4:6-7 NCV

Dear God, I know that worrying about my problems does not help anything. You are all I need. You will never let me fall. And I thank you for that, Jesus. Will you help me to learn to trust in you with all my worries?

What worries can you hand over to God today?

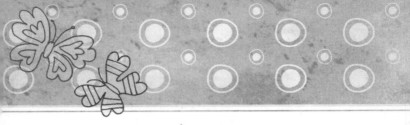

Honesty

Keep me from deceitful ways;
be gracious to me and teach me your law.
I have chosen the way of faithfulness;
I have set my heart on your laws.

PSALM 119:29-30 NIV

"Everything that is hidden will become clear,
and every secret thing will be made known."

LUKE 8:17 NCV

The king is pleased with words from righteous lips;
he loves those who speak honestly.

PROVERBS 16:13 NLT

We will speak the truth in love. So we will grow up in
every way to become the body of Christ.
Christ is the head of the body.

EPHESIANS 4:15 NIRV

Dear God, help me to always be honest. I don't want to lie to my family or friends because that is hurtful. Lying is sinful. Make me more like you, Jesus.

Is there anything you
need to be honest about?

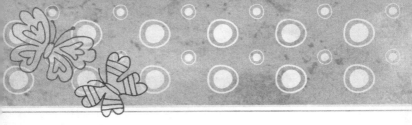

Victory

You can prepare a horse for the day of battle.
But the power to win comes from the LORD.

PROVERBS 21:31 NIRV

Every child of God defeats this evil world,
and we achieve this victory through our faith.

1 JOHN 5:4 NLT

From the LORD comes deliverance.
May your blessing be on your people.

PSALM 3:8 NIV

I love you and want to see you.
You bring me joy and make me proud of you,
so stand strong in the Lord as I have told you.

PHILIPPIANS 4:1 NCV

Dear Jesus, I am already a winner because of you!
Thank you for overcoming the world and opening your arms
to me. I hope that everything I do pleases you.

You win with Jesus in your life!
Write down your last victory.

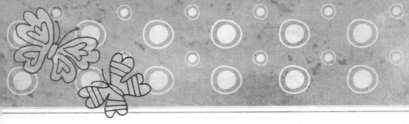

Respect

Show respect for all people: Love the brothers and sisters
of God's family, respect God, honor the king.

1 PETER 2:17 NCV

Trust in your leaders. Put yourselves under their
authority. Do this, because they keep watch over you.
They know they are accountable to God for everything
they do. Do this, so that their work will be a joy. If you
make their work a heavy load, it won't do you any good.

HEBREWS 13:17 NIRV

Don't do anything only to get ahead. Don't do it because
you are proud. Instead, be humble. Value others more
than yourselves.

PHILIPPIANS 2:3 NIRV

Dear Jesus, I pray that people can see you in me. Respecting others is important to you, so it's important to me. Part of respect is obeying, and you say to obey my leaders, like my mom, dad, and teachers. Help me to always keep that in mind.

How do you show your leaders respect?

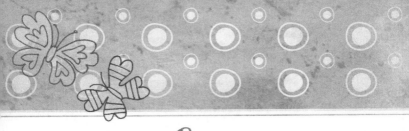

Prayer

LORD, in the morning you hear my voice.
In the morning I pray to you.
I wait for you in hope.

PSALM 5:3 NIRV

Never stop praying.

1 THESSALONIANS 5:17 NIRV

The LORD does not listen to the wicked,
but he hears the prayers of those who do right.

PROVERBS 15:29 NCV

Come, let us bow down in worship,
let us kneel before the LORD our Maker.

PSALM 95:6 NIV

Dear God, sometimes I don't talk to you as much as I should. Praying is so important! I am lucky that you love me. Thank you for hearing my prayers.

What can you pray about right now?

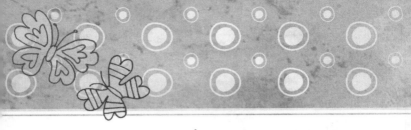

Love

Three things will last forever—faith, hope, and love—
and the greatest of these is love.

1 CORINTHIANS 13:13 NLT

LORD, you are good. You are forgiving.
You are full of love for all who call out to you.

PSALM 86:5 NIRV

Fill us with your love every morning.
Then we will sing and rejoice all our lives.

PSALM 90:14 NCV

Let love and faithfulness never leave you;
bind them around your neck,
write them on the tablet of your heart.

PROVERBS 3:3 NIV

Dear Jesus, you are a loving God. I am thankful to be your daughter. Love is about putting others before myself, so I pray that I will show love to others every day just like you do.

What is one loving thing you could do for someone else?

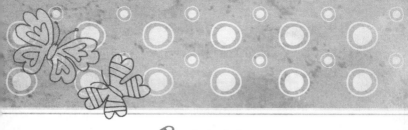

Protection

My God is my rock. I can run to him for safety. He is
my shield and my saving strength, my defender and my
place of safety. The LORD saves me from those who want
to harm me.

2 SAMUEL 22:3 NCV

The LORD keeps you from all harm
and watches over your life.
The LORD keeps watch over you as you come and go,
both now and forever.

PSALM 121:7-8 NLT

We are pushed hard from all sides. But we are not beaten
down. We are bewildered. But that doesn't make us lose
hope. Others make us suffer. But God does not desert us.
We are knocked down. But we are not knocked out.

2 CORINTHIANS 4:8-9 NIRV

Dear God, I feel safe knowing you are always watching over me. I never have to fear the evil things of this world. Thank you for being my defender. Help me to think of you the next time I am afraid.

How does it make you feel to know God is always there to protect you?

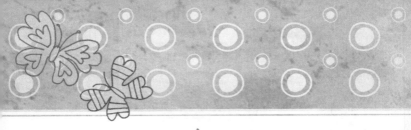

Honor

"My Father will honor the one who serves me."

JOHN 12:26 NIV

Humble yourselves under the mighty power of God,
and at the right time he will lift you up in honor.

1 PETER 5:6 NLT

Anyone who wants to be godly and loving
finds life, success and honor.

PROVERBS 21:21 NIRV

Love each other like brothers and sisters. Give each
other more honor than you want for yourselves.

ROMANS 12:10 NCV

Dear God, I pray that I honor those around me like you honor your children. Help me to be humble and kind. I want to be more like you every day.

What does it mean to honor someone else?

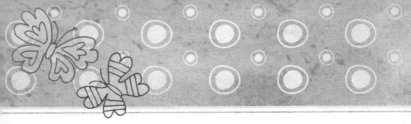

Guilt

God is faithful and fair. If we confess our sins, he will forgive our sins. He will forgive every wrong thing we have done. He will make us pure.

1 JOHN 1:9 NIRV

The LORD and King helps me. He won't let me be dishonored. So I've made up my mind to keep on serving him. I know he won't let me be put to shame.

ISAIAH 50:7 NIRV

Those who go to him for help are happy,
and they are never disgraced.

PSALM 34:5 NCV

I have not achieved it, but I focus on this one thing: Forgetting the past and looking forward to what lies ahead.

PHILIPPIANS 3:13 NLT

Dear God, help me to admit my sins so I can be forgiven. I do not want to walk around with shame and guilt about sins I have committed. My goal is to keep my heart and mind set on you.

Why doesn't God want us to feel guilt and shame?

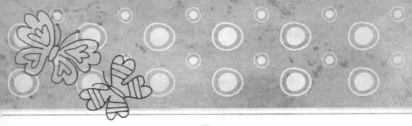

Fear

God gave us his Spirit. And the Spirit doesn't make us
weak and fearful. Instead, the Spirit gives us power and
love. He helps us control ourselves.

2 TIMOTHY 1:7 NIRV

The LORD is my light and my salvation—
whom shall I fear?
The LORD is the stronghold of my life—
of whom shall I be afraid?

PSALM 27:1 NIV

When I am afraid, I will trust you.
I praise God for his word.
I trust God, so I am not afraid.
What can human beings do to me?

PSALM 56:3-4 NCV

Dear God, thank you for giving me a spirit of power and love. That makes me feel so safe. When I do feel afraid, help me to trust in you. With you in my life, I have no one to fear.

What fears can you give to God right now?

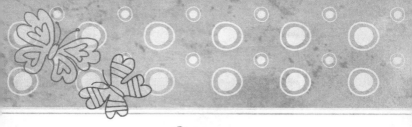

Courage

Be strong in the Lord and in his mighty power.
Put on the full armor of God, so that you can
take your stand against the devil's schemes.

EPHESIANS 6:10-11 NIV

Be alert. Continue strong in the faith.
Have courage, and be strong. Do everything in love.

1 CORINTHIANS 16:13-14 NCV

Even though I walk through the darkest valley,
I will not be afraid. You are with me.

PSALM 23:4 NIRV

"This is my command—be strong and courageous! Do
not be afraid or discouraged. For the LORD your God is
with you wherever you go."

JOSHUA 1:9 NLT

Dear God, you commanded me to always have courage. With you, I will not be discouraged or afraid. It feels good to put on the full armor of God. Thank you for being with me wherever I go.

When was the last time you showed courage?

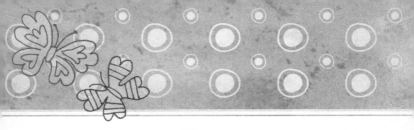

Anger

Don't get angry.
Don't be upset; it only leads to trouble.
Evil people will be sent away,
but those who trust the LORD will inherit the land.

PSALM 37:8-9 NCV

Everyone should be quick to listen, slow to speak and
slow to become angry, because human anger does not
produce the righteousness that God desires.

JAMES 1:19-20 NIV

"Don't sin by letting anger control you."
Don't let the sun go down while you are still angry.

EPHESIANS 4:26 NLT

Dear God, please help me to be slow to get angry. You want me to be patient and understanding. I pray that every night I will go to sleep with no anger in my heart toward anyone.

What does it mean to be quick to listen and slow to speak?

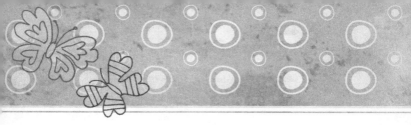

Determination

In a race all the runners run.
But only one gets the prize.
You know that, don't you?
So run in a way that will get you the prize.

1 CORINTHIANS 9:24–25 NIRV

I have tried hard to find you—
don't let me wander from your commands.

PSALM 119:10 NLT

I have fought the good fight, I have finished the race,
I have kept the faith.

2 TIMOTHY 4:7 NCV

Let us not become weary in doing good, for at the proper
time we will reap a harvest if we do not give up.

GALATIANS 6:9 NIV

Dear Jesus, I want to win. I want to win because living with you in heaven is the prize. Help me to keep trying even when I am tired. Thank you for encouraging me.

How does it make you feel
that God wants you to win?

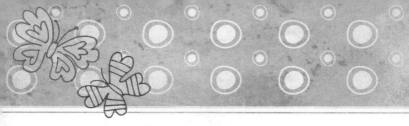

Encouragement

The LORD your God is with you;
the mighty One will save you.
He will rejoice over you.
You will rest in his love;
he will sing and be joyful about you.

ZEPHANIAH 3:17 NCV

Encourage one another daily,
as long as it is called "Today."

HEBREWS 3:13 NIV

Kind words are like honey—
sweet to the soul and healthy for the body.

PROVERBS 16:24 NLT

Be joyful. Grow to maturity. Encourage each other.
Live in harmony and peace. Then the God of love
and peace will be with you.

2 CORINTHIANS 13:11 NLT

Dear God, thank you for being so kind and loving to me. It feels good to have reminders of joy and peace. Help me to encourage my friends and family like you encourage me.

How can you encourage someone today?

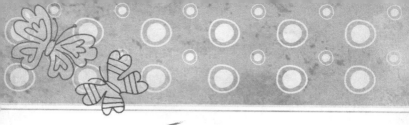

Freedom

Now the Lord is the Spirit, and where the Spirit of the
Lord is, there is freedom.

2 CORINTHIANS 3:17 NIV

My brothers and sisters, you were chosen to be free.
But don't use your freedom as an excuse to live under the
power of sin. Instead, serve one another in love.

GALATIANS 5:13 NIRV

"So if the Son sets you free, you are truly free."

JOHN 8:36 NLT

Dear Jesus, I know that you made me free so I can choose to do good. But I am a sinner, which means sometimes I choose the wrong thing. Help me live for you instead. Thank you for setting me free!

How does it feel to be free from your sin?

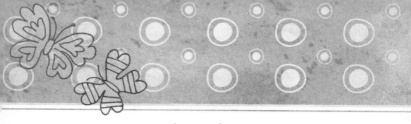

Humility

"Didn't I make everything by my power? That is how all things were created," announces the LORD. "The people I value are not proud. They are sorry for the wrong things they have done. They have great respect for what I say."

ISAIAH 66:2 NIRV

Humble yourselves before the Lord, and he will lift you up.

JAMES 4:10 NIV

Pride will ruin people, but those who are humble
will be honored.

PROVERBS 29:23 NCV

The LORD has told you what is good,
and this is what he requires of you:
to do what is right, to love mercy,
and to walk humbly with your God.

MICAH 6:8 NLT

Dear God, I want to be a person you value. Sometimes it's easier to feel selfish and prideful, but that is not right. I need to remember that all the blessings in my life come from you. Help me to be humble each day.

When is a time you acted in pride when you really should have been humble?

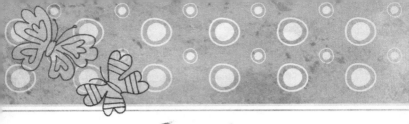

Friendship

A friend loves you all the time,
and a brother helps in time of trouble.

PROVERBS 17:17 NCV

There are "friends" who destroy each other,
but a real friend sticks closer than a brother.

PROVERBS 18:24 NLT

"Greater love has no one than this: to lay down one's
life for one's friends. You are my friends if you do what
I command.... Instead, I have called you friends, for
everything that I learned from my Father I have made
known to you."

JOHN 15:13–15 NIV

"In everything, do to others
what you would want them to do to you."

MATTHEW 7:12 NIRV

Dear God, it makes me so happy to know that I can call you a friend. You are a perfect example. My friends and I don't always get along, but help me to always treat them with love and respect.

What friend can you pray for right now?

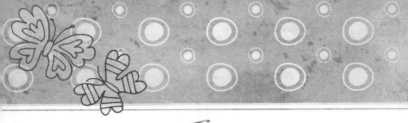

Joy

May the God of hope fill you with all joy and peace as you
trust in him, so that you may overflow with hope by the
power of the Holy Spirit.

ROMANS 15:13 NIV

"Don't be sad, because the joy of the LORD
will make you strong."

NEHEMIAH 8:10 NCV

The LORD is my strength and shield.
I trust him with all my heart.
He helps me, and my heart is filled with joy.
I burst out in songs of thanksgiving.

PSALM 28:7 NLT

Always be joyful because you belong to the Lord.
I will say it again. Be joyful!

PHILIPPIANS 4:4 NIRV

Dear Jesus, I am happy today! Thank you for being a God of love and joy. Help me to shine for you and tell others about this joy.

What is one joyful moment you had this week?

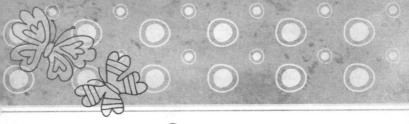

Patience

Warn those who are lazy.
Encourage those who are timid.
Take tender care of those who are weak.
Be patient with everyone.

1 Thessalonians 5:14 NLT

Be like those who through faith and patience will receive
what God has promised.

Hebrews 6:12 NCV

Be completely humble and gentle; be patient, bearing
with one another in love.

Ephesians 4:2 NIV

Anyone who is patient has great understanding. But
anyone who gets angry quickly shows how foolish they are.

Proverbs 14:29 NIRV

Dear God, it's not always easy to be patient with others. Sometimes they make me mad or take too long to do things. I want to be a kind friend and a sweet daughter. Help me to be more patient with my friends and family.

Who can you be more patient with in your life?

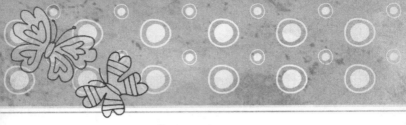

Obedience

Children, obey your parents in everything,
for this pleases the Lord.

COLOSSIANS 3:20 NIV

Even children are known by their behavior;
their actions show if they are innocent and good.

PROVERBS 20:11 NCV

Those who keep commandments keep their lives.
But those who don't care how they live will die.

PROVERBS 19:16 NIRV

Remember, it is sin to know what you ought to do
and then not do it.

JAMES 4:17 NLT

Dear God, I don't always want to do what my parents tell me. It feels unfair sometimes, but you say to obey them in everything. Help me to be good and obedient for my parents and for you.

Why does God want you
to obey your parents in everything?

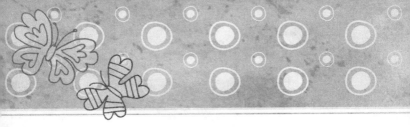

Understanding

Understanding is like a fountain of life
to those who have it.
But foolish people are punished
for the foolish things they do.

PROVERBS 16:22 NIRV

The teaching of your word gives light,
so even the simple can understand.

PSALM 119:130 NLT

Give me understanding,
so that I may keep your law
and obey it with all my heart.

PSALM 119:34 NIV

Don't act thoughtlessly, but understand
what the Lord wants you to do.

EPHESIANS 5:17 NLT

Dear God, I don't always know everything you want me to do, but I want to obey you. When I am confused and don't know where to turn, I will pray to you because I want to understand your ways and become more like you.

Is there anything you want
God's help with understanding?

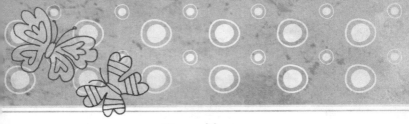

Excellence

Finally, my brothers and sisters, always think about what is true. Think about what is noble, right and pure. Think about what is lovely and worthy of respect. If anything is excellent or worthy of praise, think about those kinds of things.

PHILIPPIANS 4:8 NIRV

By his divine power, God has given us everything we need for living a godly life. We have received all of this by coming to know him, the one who called us to himself by means of his marvelous glory and excellence.

2 PETER 1:3 NLT

The answer is, if you eat or drink, or if you do anything, do it all for the glory of God.

1 CORINTHIANS 10:31 NCV

Dear God, I know that no one is perfect, but excellence
is important to you. Please help me have pure and lovely
thoughts throughout my day. I want to be the best I can be to
honor you.

In which areas would you like
to be excellent for God?

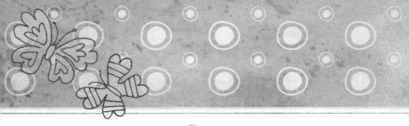

Faith

Through Christ you have come to trust in God. And you have placed your faith and hope in God because he raised Christ from the dead and gave him great glory.

1 PETER 1:21 NLT

"Because your faith is much too small. What I'm about to tell you is true. If you have faith as small as a mustard seed, it is enough. You can say to this mountain, 'Move from here to there.' And it will move. Nothing will be impossible for you."

MATTHEW 17:20 NIRV

The important thing is faith—
the kind of faith that works through love.

GALATIANS 5:6 NCV

Faith is confidence in what we hope for and assurance about what we do not see.

HEBREWS 11:1 NIV

Dear God, faith is a confusing thing. It's not something I can see or touch or hear, but it is trusting you in my heart. I know Jesus died for me so I could live with you in heaven one day. Please live in my heart today, Jesus. I want you to be with me always.

What gives you faith and hope in Jesus?

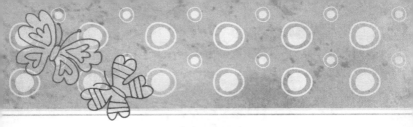

Wisdom

Wisdom will come into your mind,
and knowledge will be pleasing to you.
Good sense will protect you;
understanding will guard you.
It will keep you from the wicked,
from those whose words are bad.

PROVERBS 2:10-12 NCV

Wisdom and money can get you almost anything,
but only wisdom can save your life.

ECCLESIASTES 7:12 NLT

If any of you needs wisdom, you should ask God for it.
He will give it to you. God gives freely to everyone and
doesn't find fault.

JAMES 1:5 NIRV

Dear God, you made me into a pretty smart girl, but
there will be times in my life when I don't know what to do.
That's when I should open my ears and think before I speak.
Wisdom is asking you for help and accepting that I need you.

How can you use God's wisdom
to make better choices?

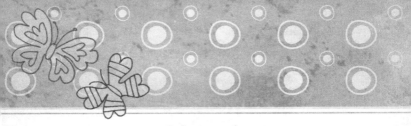

Reliability

"All people are like grass. All their glory is like the
flowers in the field. The grass dries up. The flowers fall
to the ground. But the word of the Lord lasts forever."

1 PETER 1:24-25 NIRV

Every good action and every perfect gift is from God. These
good gifts come down from the Creator of the sun, moon,
and stars, who does not change like their shifting shadows.

JAMES 1:17 NCV

You are near, LORD,
and all your commands are true.
Long ago I learned from your statutes
that you established them to last forever.

PSALM 119:151-152 NIV

Dear God, it's hard to understand that you are forever. Plants dry up when you don't water them. Pets don't live as long as the family they belong to. It's confusing. Help me to rely on you because I know I can always trust you.

How does it make you feel to know you can rely on God for anything... forever?

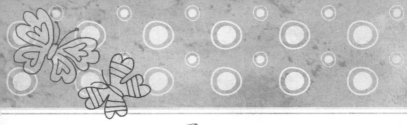

Justice

My friends, do not try to punish others when they wrong
you, but wait for God to punish them with his anger.
It is written: "I will punish those who do wrong;
I will repay them," says the Lord.

ROMANS 12:19 NCV

He is the Rock. His works are perfect. All his ways are
right. He is faithful. He doesn't do anything wrong.
He is honest and fair.

DEUTERONOMY 32:4 NIRV

The LORD secures justice for the poor
and upholds the cause of the needy.

PSALM 140:12 NIV

There is joy for those who deal justly with others
and always do what is right.

PSALM 106:3 NLT

Dear God, there are times when I want to punish those who make me feel bad. I know now that is your job. Help me to give you all my problems because you are a perfect judge.

Why is it better to let God be the judge?

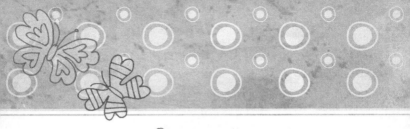

Cooperation

Make me truly happy by agreeing wholeheartedly with
each other, loving one another, and working together
with one mind and purpose.

PHILIPPIANS 2:2 NLT

Agree with one another. Don't be proud. Be willing to
be a friend of people who aren't considered important.
Don't think that you are better than others.

ROMANS 12:16 NIRV

Do not make friends with a hot-tempered person,
do not associate with one easily angered.

PROVERBS 22:24 NIV

Finally, all of you should be in agreement,
understanding each other, loving each other as family,
being kind and humble.

1 PETER 3:8 NCV

Dear God, cooperation means using others' ideas and my own to get something done. Sometimes we fight when we don't agree. I pray that you will help me to be loving and understanding, so I can work better with my friends.

Was there a time this week when you could have cooperated better?

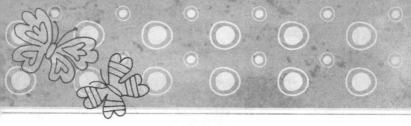

Delight

When I received your words, I ate them.
They filled me with joy. My heart took delight in them.
LORD God who rules over all, I belong to you.

JEREMIAH 15:16 NIRV

"My God, I want to do what you want.
Your teachings are in my heart."

PSALM 40:8 NCV

Your laws are my treasure;
they are my heart's delight.

PSALM 119:111 NLT

"Let your light shine before others, that they may see
your good deeds and glorify your Father in heaven."

MATTHEW 5:16 NIV

*Dear Jesus, you are in my heart, and that makes me happy!
I can't wait to keep learning about you because the more I
know, the more I love you. Thank you for being mine.*

What is your favorite part
about belonging to Jesus?

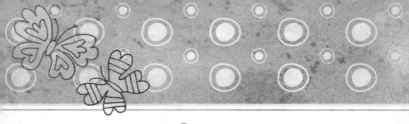

Caring

Do not be interested only in your own life, but be
interested in the lives of others.

PHILIPPIANS 2:4 NCV

If anyone has material possessions and sees a brother or
sister in need but has no pity on them, how can the love
of God be in that person? Dear children, let us not love
with words or speech but with actions and in truth.

1 JOHN 3:17-18 NIV

"I was hungry. And you gave me something to eat. I was
thirsty. And you gave me something to drink. I was a
stranger. And you invited me in. I needed clothes. And
you gave them to me. I was sick. And you took care of me.
I was in prison. And you came to visit me."

MATTHEW 25:35-36 NIRV

Dear God, I care about other people, and I want to help them. Sometimes, I only think about me—about what I want to do and when I want to do it. Help me to be more caring toward those who have less than I have.

What caring act can you do
for someone else today?

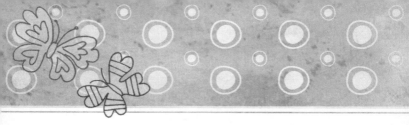

Beauty

You are altogether beautiful, my darling,
beautiful in every way.

Song of Songs 4:7 NLT

No, your beauty should come from within you—the
beauty of a gentle and quiet spirit that will never be
destroyed and is very precious to God.

1 Peter 3:4 NCV

She puts on strength and honor
as if they were her clothes.
She can laugh at the days that are coming.

Proverbs 31:25 NIRV

I praise you because you made me
in an amazing and wonderful way.
What you have done is wonderful.
I know this very well.

Psalm 139:14 NCV

Dear God, I don't always feel beautiful, but you made me, so I know I am wonderful. Help me to work on beautifying my heart for you because my inside is more important than my outward appearance.

How does it make you feel that Jesus calls you beautiful in every way?

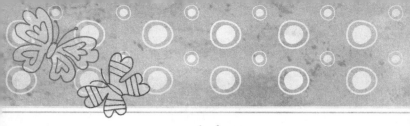

Help

My brothers and sisters, you will face all kinds of trouble.
When you do, think of it as pure joy. Your faith will be
tested. You know that when this happens it will produce
in you the strength to continue.

JAMES 1:2-3 NIRV

God will never forget the needy;
the hope of the afflicted will never perish.

PSALM 9:18 NIV

So take a new grip with your tired hands and strengthen
your weak knees. Mark out a straight path for your feet
so that those who are weak and lame will not fall but
become strong.

HEBREWS 12:12-14 NLT

"My grace is enough for you. When you are weak,
my power is made perfect in you."

2 CORINTHIANS 12:9 NCV

Dear God, sometimes I feel like I can't do anything. I'm too tired. I'm too weak. You say I should be happy about those times because it's then I know I need you. Thank you for being my strength.

Was there anything you were unable to do this week without God's help?

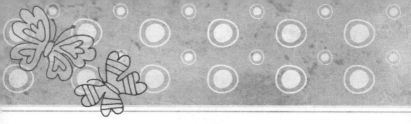

Eternity

We are citizens of heaven,
where the Lord Jesus Christ lives.
And we are eagerly waiting for him to return as our Savior.

PHILIPPIANS 3:20 NLT

"And if I go and prepare a place for you,
I will come back and take you to be with me
that you also may be where I am."

JOHN 14:3 NIV

That will happen in a flash, as quickly as you can wink an
eye. It will happen at the blast of the last trumpet. Then the
dead will be raised to live forever. And we will be changed.

1 CORINTHIANS 15:52 NIRV

Surely your goodness and love will be with me all my life,
and I will live in the house of the LORD forever.

PSALM 23:6 NCV

Dear Jesus, living forever is hard to imagine. It's kind of scary to think about sometimes. But living forever with you is exciting. Help me to understand what eternity means and how great a gift it is.

What questions do you have
about eternity and heaven?

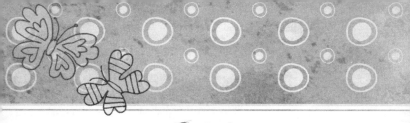

Family

Jesus, who makes people holy, and those who are made holy are from the same family. So he is not ashamed to call them his brothers and sisters.

HEBREWS 2:11 NCV

Therefore, as we have opportunity, let us do good to all people, especially to those who belong to the family of believers.

GALATIANS 6:10 NIV

So it is with Christ's body. We are many parts of one body, and we all belong to each other.

ROMANS 12:5 NLT

Dear God, my family is bigger than just the people I live with. I am your daughter; you are my father. I have a whole other family with all your children in the world. Thank you for making me part of something bigger.

What do you think about having so many family members who love Jesus?

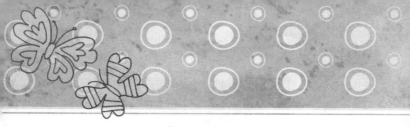

Happiness

I will praise you, LORD, with all my heart.
I will tell all the miracles you have done.
I will be happy because of you;
God Most High, I will sing praises to your name.

PSALM 9:1-2 NCV

LORD, you alone are my inheritance, my cup of blessing.
You guard all that is mine.
The land you have given me is a pleasant land. What a
wonderful inheritance!

PSALM 16:5-6 NLT

Happiness makes a person smile,
but sadness can break a person's spirit.

PROVERBS 15:13 NCV

People should be happy and do good while they live.
I know there's nothing better for them to do than that.

ECCLESIASTES 3:12 NIRV

Dear God, you like when I am happy. I pray that when I'm feeling sad I can remember the blessings you have given me and smile because you are in my heart. Help me to smile more and do good.

What are you happy about right now?

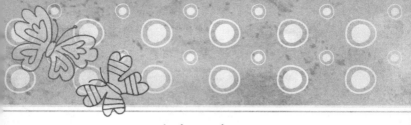

Helpfulness

"In everything I did, I showed you that by this kind of hard work we must help the weak, remembering the words the Lord Jesus himself said: 'It is more blessed to give than to receive.'"

ACTS 20:35 NIV

"Who is more important? Is it the one at the table, or the one who serves? Isn't it the one who is at the table? But I am among you as one who serves."

LUKE 22:27 NIRV

Share with God's people who need help. Bring strangers in need into your homes.

ROMANS 12:13 NCV

Dear Jesus, I want to serve others just like you. You say it is better to give than receive. I pray that I will become more helpful to my friends, family, and others in need.

What is something helpful you could do for your family?

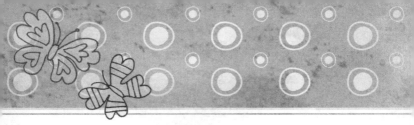

Praise

Sing to the LORD a new song,
his praise from the ends of the earth,
you who go down to the sea, and all that is in it, you
islands, and all who live in them.

ISAIAH 42:10 NIV

Praise the LORD from the skies.
Praise him high above the earth.
Praise him, all you angels.
Praise him, all you armies of heaven.
Praise him, sun and moon.
Praise him, all you shining stars.
Praise him, highest heavens
and you waters above the sky.
Let them praise the LORD,
because they were created by his command.

PSALM 148:1–5 NCV

Dear God, thank you for sending your Son to die for me.
Thank you for living in my heart and being with me always.
Thank you for my family and my friends. You deserve all my
praise and more.

What is something specific
you can praise God for today?

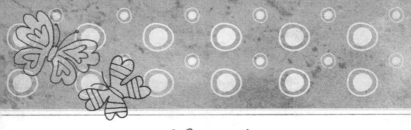

Reward

Work willingly at whatever you do, as though you were
working for the Lord rather than for people. Remember
that the Lord will give you an inheritance as your reward,
and that the Master you are serving is Christ.

COLOSSIANS 3:23-24 NLT

"Love your enemies, do good to them, and lend to them
without expecting to get anything back. Then your
reward will be great, and you will be children of the Most
High, because he is kind to the ungrateful and wicked."

LUKE 6:35 NIV

Without faith it is impossible to please God. Those who
come to God must believe that he exists. And they must
believe that he rewards those who look to him.

HEBREWS 11:6 NIRV

Dear God, thank you for the rewards you give me when I am obedient to you. Help me to keep being kind and loving toward others. I want you to be proud of me.

Has God ever rewarded you for work you did?

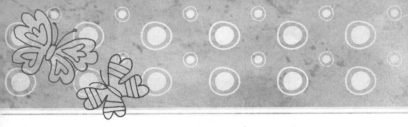

Strength

God is our refuge and strength,
an ever-present help in trouble.

PSALM 46:1-3 NIV

The Lord is faithful; he will strengthen you and guard
you from the evil one.

2 THESSALONIANS 3:3 NIRV

Don't be afraid, for I am with you.
Don't be discouraged, for I am your God.
I will strengthen you and help you.
I will hold you up with my victorious right hand.

ISAIAH 41:10 NLT

Dear God, when I hear things like, "You hit like a girl,"
or, "You throw like a girl," I don't feel very strong. I need
to remember the strength you constantly give me. I can do
anything with you in my heart. Thank you for picking me up
and helping me be strong.

What makes you feel strong?

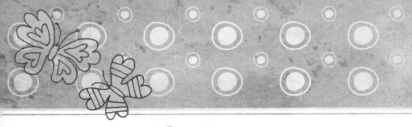

Temptation

The temptations in your life are no different
from what others experience. And God is faithful.
He will not allow the temptation to be more
than you can stand. When you are tempted,
he will show you a way out so that you can endure.

1 Corinthians 10:13 NLT

"Watch and pray so that you will not fall into temptation.
The spirit is willing, but the flesh is weak."

Matthew 26:41 NIV

I have taken your words to heart
so I would not sin against you.

Psalm 119:11 NCV

Dear God, there are temptations in this world. Temptations to cheat, or lie, or take things that don't belong to me. If I am tempted to do bad things, I pray you will help me choose the right thing to do instead.

What temptations have you felt before?

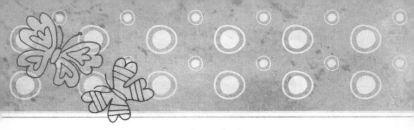

Health

The world and its desires pass away,
but whoever does the will of God lives forever.

1 JOHN 2:17 NIV

Don't be wise in your own eyes.
Have respect for the LORD and avoid evil.
That will bring health to your body.
It will make your bones strong.

PROVERBS 3:7-8 NIRV

I will never forget your commandments,
for by them you give me life.

PSALM 119:93 NLT

A happy heart is like good medicine,
but a broken spirit drains your strength.

PROVERBS 17:22 NCV

Dear God, people get sick every day. Their bodies and their hearts can get sick, but you are a healer. I pray that I follow you always and continue to ask you for health for me and for those around me.

How can you make sure your body
and your heart are healthy?

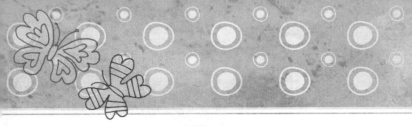

Trust

Those who know the LORD trust him,
because he will not leave those who come to him.

PSALM 9:10 NCV

I trust in you, LORD. I say, "You are my God."
My whole life is in your hands.
Save me from the hands of my enemies.
Save me from those who are chasing me.

PSALM 31:14–15 NIV

Yes, the LORD is for me; he will help me.
I will look in triumph at those who hate me.
It is better to take refuge in the LORD
than to trust in people.

PSALM 118:7–8 NLT

Dear Jesus, you are the truth. I know I can trust in you even when I can't trust this world or the people in it. Help me to look to you when I am in need.

How do you know that God is trustworthy?

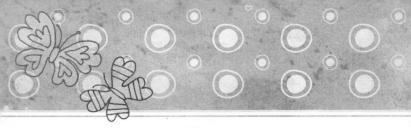

Quiet

There is a time to tear apart and a time to sew together.
There is a time to be silent and a time to speak.

ECCLESIASTES 3:7 NCV

It is good to wait quietly for salvation from the LORD.

LAMENTATIONS 3:26 NLT

Those who are careful about what they say
keep themselves out of trouble.

PROVERBS 21:23 NIRV

Tremble and do not sin;
when you are on your beds,
search your hearts and be silent.

PSALM 4:4 NIV

Dear God, it's easy to fill my head with noise. I like to listen to music, to talk with my friends, to watch movies. I need help learning to be silent so I can hear your voice.

When was the last time you were quiet enough to listen to God?

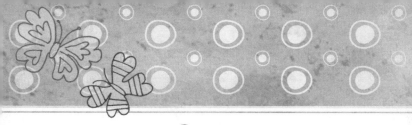

Purpose

You have been raised up with Christ. So think about
things that are in heaven. That is where Christ is.
He is sitting at God's right hand.

COLOSSIANS 3:1 NIRV

We know that in all things God works for the good of
those who love him, who have been called according
to his purpose.

ROMANS 8:28 NIV

My child, pay attention to my words;
listen closely to what I say.
Don't ever forget my words;
keep them always in mind.

PROVERBS 4:20-21 NCV

Dear God, help me to focus on you. My job is to think about what you teach and share it with others. Show me the purpose you have for me, and help me to stay close to you so it can come about.

How do you feel when you think about God having a special purpose for your life?

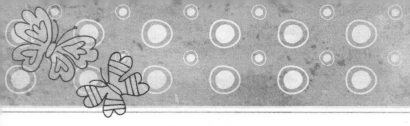

Kindness

Be kind to each other, tenderhearted, forgiving one
another, just as God through Christ has forgiven you.

EPHESIANS 4:32 NLT

Kind people do themselves a favor,
but cruel people bring trouble on themselves.

PROVERBS 11:17 NCV

Do you disrespect God's great kindness and favor?
Do you disrespect God when he is patient with you?
Don't you realize that God's kindness is meant
to turn you away from your sins?

ROMANS 2:4 NIRV

For great is his love toward us,
and the faithfulness of the LORD endures forever.
Praise the LORD.

PSALM 117:2 NIV

Dear Jesus, it's not always easy to be kind to everyone,
but I know that even when I don't deserve it, you will call me
your precious daughter. Help me to use your example to be
kind in everything I do.

What is the last act of kindness
someone showed you?

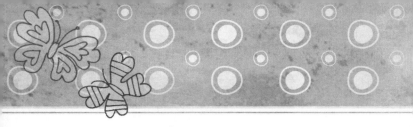

Learning

Those who get wisdom do themselves a favor,
and those who love learning will succeed.

PROVERBS 19:8 NCV

Pay attention to my wisdom;
listen carefully to my wise counsel.
Then you will show discernment,
and your lips will express what you've learned.

PROVERBS 5:1-2 NLT

Hold on to my teaching and don't let it go.
Guard it well, because it is your life.

PROVERBS 4:13 NIRV

Whatever you have learned or received
or heard from me, or seen in me—put it into practice.
And the God of peace will be with you.

PHILIPPIANS 4:9 NIV

Dear God, I don't always love doing homework, but I do love learning. You say to listen and hold on to what I've learned, so I will. Help me to use what I learn to be more like you every day.

What is your favorite part of learning?

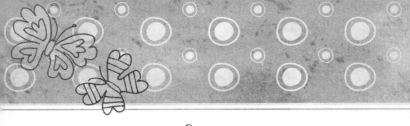

Grace

Let the words you speak always be full of grace.
Learn how to make your words what people want to hear.
Then you will know how to answer everyone.

COLOSSIANS 4:6 NIRV

God gives us even more grace, as the Scripture says, "God
is against the proud, but he gives grace to the humble."

JAMES 4:6 NCV

Sin is no longer your master, for you no longer live
under the requirements of the law. Instead, you live
under the freedom of God's grace.

ROMANS 6:14 NLT

Dear God, I want to be a perfect daughter for you, but we both know that's not possible. Your grace means you love me even though I am a sinner. Thank you for wanting me when I don't deserve it.

What does grace look like in your life?

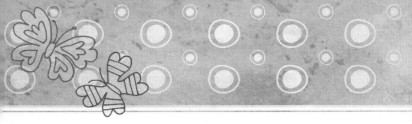

Discouragement

"For I know the plans I have for you," declares the LORD,
"plans to prosper you and not to harm you,
plans to give you hope and a future."

JEREMIAH 29:11 NIV

"Come to me, all of you who are tired and have heavy
loads, and I will give you rest."

MATTHEW 11:28 NCV

This same God who takes care of me will
supply all your needs from his glorious riches,
which have been given to us in Christ Jesus.

PHILIPPIANS 4:19 NLT

Dear God, thank you for building me up when I don't feel confident. Some days, I feel discouraged. Maybe I messed up a project or got a bad grade. Help me not to give up, and instead ask you for hope.

Do you ask God for help
when you're discouraged?

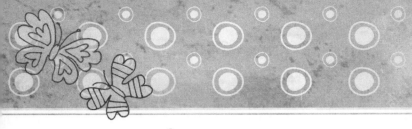

Generosity

Give generously to them and do so without a grudging
heart; then because of this the LORD your God will bless you
in all your work and in everything you put your hand to.

DEUTERONOMY 15:10 NIV

Each of you should give what you have decided in your
heart to give. You shouldn't give if you don't want to.
You shouldn't give because you are forced to.
God loves a cheerful giver.

2 CORINTHIANS 9:7 NIRV

If you help the poor, you are lending to the LORD—
and he will repay you!

PROVERBS 19:17 NLT

Dear God, it feels good to give to others, like when I share my food or clothes. It feels even better knowing that when I help others, I am helping you! I want to be a cheerful giver. Help me to give generously.

How do you feel when you share with others?

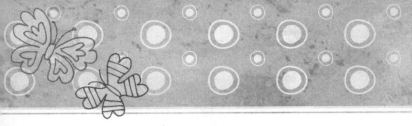

Devotion

Then Jesus said to his disciples, "Whoever wants to be
my disciple must deny themselves and take up their
cross and follow me."

MATTHEW 16:24 NIV

"No servant can serve two masters. The servant will hate
one master and love the other, or will follow one master
and refuse to follow the other. You cannot serve both God
and worldly riches."

LUKE 16:13 NCV

Do your best to please God.
Be a worker who doesn't need to be ashamed.
Teach the message of truth correctly.

2 TIMOTHY 2:15 NIRV

Dear God, devotion to you means love, loyalty, and praise for you. You have given me a lot to be thankful for in this world, but I pray that I remember to keep my eyes on you. You are more important than anything.

How can you devote your life more to God?

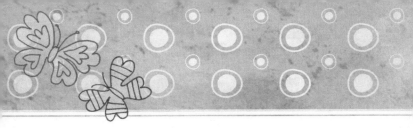

Creativity

Lord, you have made many things;
with your wisdom you made them all.
The earth is full of your riches.

PSALM 104:24 NCV

We are God's masterpiece. He has created us anew in
Christ Jesus, so we can do the good things he planned for
us long ago.

EPHESIANS 2:10 NLT

The Lord has filled him with the Spirit of God.
He has filled him with wisdom, with understanding,
with knowledge and with all kinds of skill.

EXODUS 35:31 NIRV

We have different gifts,
according to the grace given to each of us.

ROMANS 12:6 NIV

Dear God, you are such a wonderful artist. You created all the pretty colors and all the different faces in this world. Help me to be creative and start using the gifts you've given me.

How can you use your creativity for God?

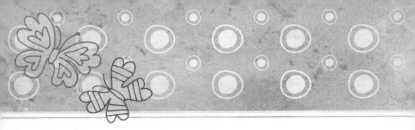

Guidance

Guide me in your truth and teach me,
for you are God my Savior,
and my hope is in you all day long.

PSALM 25:5 NIV

Wise people can also listen and learn;
even they can find good advice in these words.

PROVERBS 1:5 NCV

We can make our plans,
but the LORD determines our steps.

PROVERBS 16:9 NLT

Those who are led by the Spirit of God
are children of God.

ROMANS 8:14 NIRV

Dear God, sometimes I want to do everything myself. I often think I know what's best for me. Help me to stop thinking that way because you are the one who should guide my steps and my life.

Is there anything God can help guide you in today?

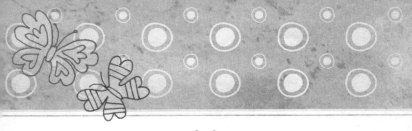

Life

All praise to God, the Father of our Lord Jesus Christ.
It is by his great mercy that we have been born again,
because God raised Jesus Christ from the dead.
Now we live with great expectation.

1 PETER 1:3 NLT

That faith and that knowledge come from the hope for life
forever, which God promised to us before time began.

TITUS 1:2 NCV

"I am the way and the truth and the life.
No one comes to the Father except through me."

JOHN 14:6 NIRV

Dear God, thank you for the life you have given me. I am so happy you are with me in my heart because I get to live forever! I pray that I use everything you have given me to please you.

What is your favorite part of life?

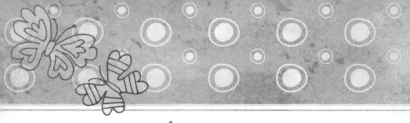

Integrity

I know, my God, that you test the heart and are pleased
with integrity. All these things I have given willingly and
with honest intent.

1 Chronicles 29:17 NIV

"So if you ignore the least commandment and teach others
to do the same, you will be called the least in the Kingdom
of Heaven. But anyone who obeys God's laws and teaches
them will be called great in the Kingdom of Heaven."

Matthew 5:19 NLT

The honest person will live in safety,
but the dishonest will be caught.

Proverbs 10:9 NCV

Dear God, living with integrity means being honest and pure at all times. I know I am not perfect, but I know how you want me to live. Help me to be a good example of integrity to my friends and family.

What does integrity mean to you?

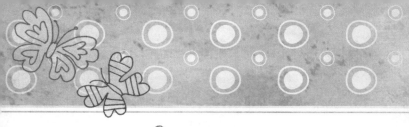

Compassion

When I am with those who are weak, I share their
weakness, for I want to bring the weak to Christ.
Yes, I try to find common ground with everyone,
doing everything I can to save some.

1 CORINTHIANS 9:22 NLT

God, have mercy on me according to your faithful love.
Because your love is so tender and kind, wipe out my
lawless acts.

PSALM 51:1 NIRV

Praise be to the God and Father of our Lord Jesus Christ,
the Father of compassion and the God of all comfort.

2 CORINTHIANS 1:3 NIV

Dear God, thank you for being compassionate with me.
It feels so good to know you want to share in my troubles.
Guide me to have compassion for my friends and family,
so I can show them the love you show me.

How can you be a more compassionate friend?

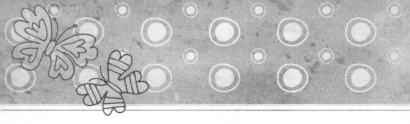

Goodness

Everything God created is good, and nothing is to be
rejected if it is received with thanksgiving.

1 Timothy 4:4 NIV

Taste and see that the Lord is good.
Oh, the joys of those who take refuge in him!

Psalm 34:8 NLT

My brothers and sisters, I am sure that you are full of
goodness. I know that you have all the knowledge you
need and that you are able to teach each other.

Romans 15:14 NCV

Dear God, sometimes school work is frustrating or my family bugs me. I know you created me to be good and share that goodness with others. Even if it's not always easy to do that, I pray that others will see your goodness in me.

What's hard about being good all the time?

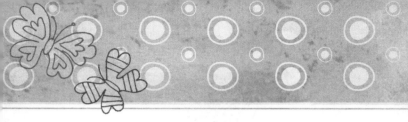

Light

"I am the light of the world. Whoever follows me will never walk in darkness, but will have the light of life."

JOHN 8:12 NIV

"You are the light of the world—like a city on a hilltop that cannot be hidden. No one lights a lamp and then puts it under a basket. Instead, a lamp is placed on a stand, where it gives light to everyone in the house. In the same way, let your good deeds shine out for all to see, so that everyone will praise your heavenly Father."

MATTHEW 5:14-16 NLT

At one time you were in the dark. But now you are in the light because of what the Lord has done. Live like children of the light.

EPHESIANS 5:8 NIRV

Dear Jesus, because of you, I live in light instead of darkness. I don't want my friends to be in the dark, so I should let them see my light! Help me to be confident in sharing the good news with them.

How can you be a brighter light for Jesus?

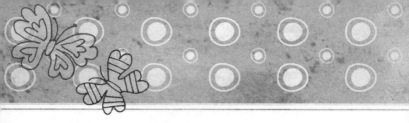

Anxiety

You will keep in perfect peace those whose minds are
steadfast, because they trust in you.

ISAIAH 26:3 NIV

"Don't let your hearts be troubled.
Trust in God, and trust also in me."

JOHN 14:1 NLT

Give all your worries to him,
because he cares about you.

1 PETER 5:7 NCV

I call out to the LORD when I'm in trouble,
and he answers me.

PSALM 120:1 NIRV

Dear God, I need to learn to trust in you more because you care about me and my troubles. Tests make me anxious, but I don't ever need to feel that way. Help me to reach out to you the next time I feel anxious.

What steps can you take to be less anxious and more trusting?

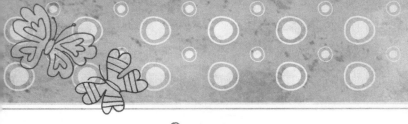

Courtesy

Each of us should please our neighbors for their good,
to build them up. For even Christ did not please himself
but, as it is written: "The insults of those who insult you
have fallen on me."

ROMANS 15:2-3 NIV

Welcome strangers, because some who have done this
have welcomed angels without knowing it.

HEBREWS 13:2 NCV

Remind God's people to obey rulers and authorities.
Remind them to be ready to do what is good. Tell them
not to speak evil things against anyone. Remind them to
live in peace. They must consider the needs of others.
They must always be gentle toward everyone.

TITUS 3:1-2 NIRV

Dear God, courtesy means being polite and thoughtful and putting others before myself. It's not only friends and family that I should be courteous toward. You say strangers could be angels, so I should be gentle and loving to everyone.

Why isn't it easy to put others' needs before your own?

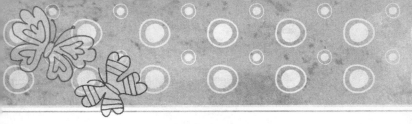

Boldness

He proclaimed the kingdom of God and taught
about the Lord Jesus Christ—with all boldness
and without hindrance!

Acts 28:31 niv

Sinners run away even when no one is chasing them.
But those who do what is right are as bold as lions.

Proverbs 28:1 nirv

On the day I called you, you answered me.
You made me strong and brave.

Psalm 138:3 ncv

So let us come boldly to the throne of our gracious God.
There we will receive his mercy, and we will find grace to
help us when we need it most.

Hebrews 4:16 nlt

Dear God, sometimes I want to be quiet and unseen, but you want me to be a bold girl of Christ! Since you have given me strength and confidence, I pray that you help me tell my friends about you boldly.

Why is it sometimes hard to be bold?

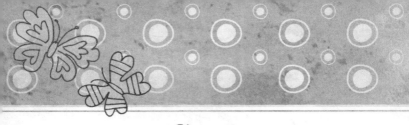

Change

"Truly I tell you, unless you change and become like little children, you will never enter the kingdom of heaven."

MATTHEW 18:3 NIV

Look! I tell you this secret: We will not all sleep in death, but we will all be changed.

1 CORINTHIANS 15:51 NCV

He will take our weak mortal bodies and change them into glorious bodies like his own, using the same power with which he will bring everything under his control.

PHILIPPIANS 3:21 NLT

Jesus Christ is the same yesterday and today and forever.

HEBREWS 13:8 NIRV

Dear God, I cannot wait to be changed by you. I am excited and a little nervous for that day, but I feel better knowing you will never change. You and your promises are forever and ever.

What does becoming like little children mean?

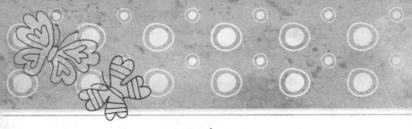

Gentleness

"Accept my teachings and learn from me,
because I am gentle and humble in spirit,
and you will find rest for your lives."

MATTHEW 11:29 NCV

"Blessed are those who are humble.
They will be given the earth."

MATTHEW 5:5 NIRV

A gentle answer turns away wrath,
but a harsh word stirs up anger.

PROVERBS 15:1 NIV

Some people have gone astray without knowing it.
He is able to deal gently with them.

HEBREWS 5:2 NIRV

Dear God, I admire how gentle you are with your children. I want to treat others with the same gentleness. It's true that arguments go much more peacefully when answers are gentle instead of harsh. Help me to remember that.

What are some steps you can take
to become more gentle?

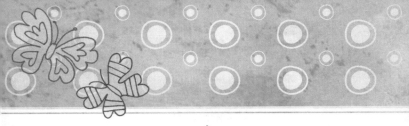

Loneliness

"Teach them to obey everything that I have taught you, and
I will be with you always, even until the end of this age."

MATTHEW 28:20 NCV

The LORD is near to all who call on him,
yes, to all who call on him in truth.

PSALM 145:18 NLT

Who can separate us from Christ's love?
Can trouble or hard times or harm or hunger?
Can nakedness or danger or war?

ROMANS 8:35 NIRV

"Be strong and courageous. Do not be afraid or terrified
because of them, for the LORD your God goes with you;
he will never leave you nor forsake you."

DEUTERONOMY 31:6 NIV

Dear God, sometimes I feel lonely, but it's nice to know I am never truly alone even if my family is not around. I have nothing to be sad about or afraid of because you are right next to me all the time.

When do you feel lonely?

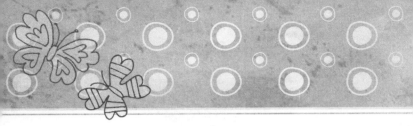

Belief

To all who believed him and accepted him,
he gave the right to become children of God.

The message as it has been taught can be trusted. He
must hold firmly to it. Then he will be able to use true
teaching to comfort others and build them up. He will be
able to prove that people who oppose it are wrong.

Dear Jesus, thank you for dying for me. I believe in you and want to live for you every day. Help me to learn as much as I can about you in case I ever need to defend your name.

When did you start believing in Jesus?

BroadStreet Kids
BroadStreet Kids is an imprint of BroadStreet Publishing Group, LLC.
Racine, Wisconsin, USA
Broadstreetpublishing.com

Prayers AND Promises for Girls

ISBN 978-1-4245-5661-8

Design by Chris Garborg | garborgdesign.com
Compiled by Kendall Moon.
Edited by Michelle Winger.

Printed in the USA.

18 19 20 21 22 23 24   7 6 5 4 3 2 1